Language Lesson 4

Finding and Understanding the Word

SonLight Education Ministry
United States of America

A Suggested Daily Schedule

(Adapt this schedule to your family needs.)

5:00 a.m.  Arise–Personal Worship

6:00 a.m. Family Worship and Bible Class–With Father

7:00 a.m. Breakfast

8:00 a.m. Practical Arts*–Domestic Activities
Agriculture
Industrial Arts
(especially those related to
the School Lessons)

10:00 a.m. School Lessons
(Take a break for some physical exercise
during this time slot.)

12:00 p.m. Dinner Preparations
(Health class could be included at this time
or a continued story.)

1:00 p.m. Dinner

2:00 p.m. Practical Arts* or Fine Arts
(Music and Crafts)
(especially those related to
the School Lessons)

5:00 p.m. Supper

6:00 p.m. Family Worship–Father
(Could do History Class)

7:00 p.m. Personal time with God–Bed Preparation

8:00 p.m. Bed

*Daily nature walk can be in morning or afternoon.

The Desire of All Nations

This book is a part of a curriculum that is built upon the life of Christ entitled, "The Desire of All Nations," for grades 2-8. Any of the books in this curriculum can be used by themselves or as an entire program.

INFORMATION ABOUT THE 2-8 GRADE PROGRAM

Multi-level

This program is written on a multi-level. That means that each booklet has material for grades 2-8. This is so the whole family in these grades may work from the same books. It is difficult for a busy mother to have 2 or more children and each have a different set of books. Remember, the Bible is written for all ages.

The Bible—the Primary Textbook

The books in this program are designed to teach the parent and the student how to learn academic subjects by using the Bible as a primary textbook.

The Desire of Ages

The Desire of Ages by Ellen G. White is used as a textbook to go with the Bible. This focuses on the early life of Christ, when He was a child. Children relate best to Christ as a child and youth.

Lesson Numbers

The big number in the top right corner on the cover of this book is the Lesson Number and corresponds with the chapter number in the book *The Desire of Ages*. For example, Lesson 1 in the school program will go along with chapter 1 in *The Desire of Ages*. Usually each family starts at the beginning with Lesson 1. Most children have not had a true Bible program, therefore they need the foundation built. If there is academic material that they have already covered, they do the Bible part and review then pass quickly on.

Seven Academic Subjects

There are seven academic subjects in this program—Health, Mathematics, Music, Science–Nature, History/Geography/Prophecy, Language, Voice–Speech.

Language Program

A good, solid language program is recommended to be used along with the SonLight materials.

The Riggs Institute has a multi-sensory teaching method that accommodates every child's unique learning style. Their program is called *Writing and Spelling Road to Reading and Thinking*. Order by calling (800) 200-4840 or visit www.riggsinst.org. (Disclaimer: SonLight does not endorse the reading books recommended in the Riggs' program.)

Another option which you might find more user friendly and is similar to the Riggs program but from a Christian perspective is *Spell to Write and Read* by Wanda Sanseri. To order, call Wanda Sanseri at (503) 654-2300 or visit https://www.bhibooks.net/swr.html

"Unto You a Saviour"
Lesson 4 – Humbleness

**The following books are those you will need for this lesson.
All of these can be obtained from www.sonlighteducation.com**

The Rainbow Covenant – Study the spiritual meaning of colors and make your own rainbow book.

Health
The Bladder

Math
Addition II

Music
The Staff, Grand Staff, and Lines

Science/Nature
Space Exploration

A Casket – Coloring book and story. Learn how to treat the gems of the Bible.

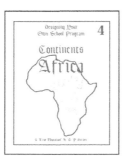

H/G/P
Africa

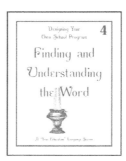

Language
Finding and Understanding the Word

Speech/Voice
The Principle of Breathing

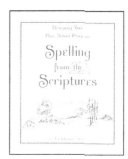

Spelling from the Scriptures

Bible Study – Learn how to study the Bible and helpful use tools.

Bible
The Desire of all Nations I
Teacher Study Guide

Student Study Guide

Bible Lesson Study Guide

Memory Verses
The Desire of all Nations I
Scripture Songs Book

and MP3 files

Our Nature Study Book – Your personal nature journal.

Table of Contents

Table of Contents

The Bible

A glory gilds the sacred page
Majestic like the sun;
It gives a light to every age,
It gives, but borrows none.
—*Cowper*

Teacher
Section

"But sanctify the Lord God in your hearts: and be ready always to give an answer to every man that asketh you a reason of the hope that is in you with meekness and fear."

I Peter 3:15

INSTRUCTIONS
For the Teacher

Step 1

Study the Bible Lesson and begin to memorize the Memory Verses. Familiarize Yourself With the Character Quality. The student can answer the Bible Review Questions. See page 7. Use the Steps in Bible Study.

Bible Lesson

"Unto You a Saviour" – Luke 2:1-20

Memory Verses

Isaiah 44:3; Psalm 112:4;
Luke 2:10-14; Romans 11:33

Character Quality

Humbleness – freedom from pride and arrogance; humility of mind; a modest estimate of one's own worth; lowliness of mind; a deep sense of one's own unworthiness in the sight of God; self-abasement; penitence for sin, and submission to divine will.

Antonyms – pride; arrogance; insolence; haughtiness; disdain; vainness; vainglory; ostentation; pretension; showiness; exaltation; aggradizement

Character Quality Verse

James 4:6 – *"But he giveth more grace. Wherefore he saith, God resisteth the proud, but giveth grace unto the **humble**."*

Step 2

Understand How To/And

A. Do the Spelling Cards so the student can begin to build his own spiritual dictionary.

B. Mark Your Bible.

C. Evaluate Your Student's Character in relation to the character quality of **humbleness**.

D. Familiarize Yourself With Language. Notice the Projects.

E. Review the Scripture References for Language.

F. Notice the Answer Key.

A. Spelling Cards

Spelling Lists

Language Words
Place I - II - III
clarity
counsel
guide
noble
understand

Place II - III
chamber
important
storehouse
understanding

Place III
audience
Bereans

Bible Words
angels
babe
Bethlehem
born
circumcising
clothes
decree
eight

Bible Words
continued
flock
firstborn
Galilee
glory
haste
heaven
humbleness
Joseph
joy
lineage
Lord
manger
Mary
multitude
Nazareth
night
peace
praising
Saviour
shepherds
shone
swaddling
taxed
tidings
will
wrapped

B. How to Mark the Bible

1. Copy the list of Bible texts in the back of the Bible on an empty page as a guide.

2. Go to the first text in the Bible and copy the next text beside it. Go to the next one and repeat the process until they are all chain-referenced.

3. Have the student present the study to family and/or friends.

4. Each student lesson contains one or more sections that have a Bible marking study on the subject studied. (See the Student's Section, page 21.)

C. Evaluate Your Student's Character

This section is for the purpose of helping the teacher know how to encourage the students to become more **humble**.

See page 8.

See the book
Spelling from the Scriptures
for instructions about how to make the Spelling Cards.

Place I = Grades 2-3-4
Place II = Grades 4-5-6
Place III = Grades 6-7-8

D. Familiarize Yourself
With "Finding and Understanding the Word"
– Notice the Projects
Projects

1. During these lessons about **humbleness** encourage your child to take the **humblest** job or the job no one else wants. (Example: scrubbing the toilets) Remind your student of things he learned in the resource materials as you were studying the Bible Lesson, "Unto You a Saviour."

2. As a family, learn to use the *Strong's Exhaustive Concordance.*

3. On your nature walks, gather live things for further study. Use your tools from your backpack. Find the lesson of **humbleness** in these objects keeping the Bible Lesson in mind. (Example: As you see the tiny creatures on your nature walk such as the ants, imagine how it would be if you had to become an ant forever—to take on their nature and live among them when you had known a higher type of life as a person. Thinking about such things might help you appreciate the **humble** position Jesus took by being born into the human family.

He will keep the human form throughout eternity, and so it is an infinite sacrifice. One can only wonder how much it has limited Him. Eternity alone will reveal to us what He has given up for our sakes.) Record your information in *Our Nature Study Book.*

4. Visit a hospital, or a friend with a newborn, and, as you look at the newborn babies, think how Jesus once was that tiny. Discuss how Jesus was received when He came to this earth. How is it different or similar to what happens when there is a birth in the family in our times?

5. As you use a scoop to dish out the dog food, be reminded how the concordance is a tool you can use to help you go deeper in God's Word.

6. Have the student use his memory verses and look up words from them for more understanding. He can write out what he finds on a piece of paper.

Example of Looking Up a Word
From the Memory Verse

Isaiah 44:3 – *"For I will pour water upon him that is thirsty, and floods upon the dry ground: I will pour my spirit upon thy seed, and my blessing upon thine offspring."*

1. Look up *"Blessing"* in the main part of the concordance.

2. Find the number to the right of the word (1293).

3. Go to the proper dictionary in the back of the concordance. Use the Hebrew dictionary for Isaiah 44:3 – *"Blessing"*

    Old Testament – Hebrew Dictionary
    New Testament – Greek Dictionary

4. Especially notice the words in italics as they are the final definition.

    Example:

    1293 – *"Blessing"* – benediction; prosperity

5. Write down the meaning of the word *"Blessing"* found in italics. Discuss the meaning.

6. Do page 7 in the booklet *Bible Study*.

Sweet Words

In India a man received a package wrapped in portions of the Scriptures. Later he wrote a Christian friend saying: "I bought some sweets and through the message printed on the paper in which they were wrapped in found the sweetness of forgiveness of sins."

E. Review the References for Language

Teacher, read through this section before working on the lesson with the student. See page 21 in the Student Section.

F. Notice the Answer Key

The Answer Key for the student book is found on page 9.

Step 3

Read the Lesson Aim.

Lesson Aim

This lesson will help to teach the child how **humble** Jesus was to come to this earth and take such a lowly position. The child will be studying more information about Jesus' birth through resource materials. Just as the Father sent Jesus to *"save his people from their sins"*

(Matthew 1:21), so today He sends the Word to save us from our sins. *"And he sent his word, and healed them, and delivered them from their destructions"* (Psalm 107:20). *"Thy word have I hid in mine heart that I might not sin against thee"* (Psalm 119:11).

This lesson will help the child learn how to use a *Strong's Concordance* to understand what certain words mean. The concordance is one of the best tools used to dig deep in Bible study. It will help you to *"study to shew thyself approved unto God, a workman that needeth not to be ashamed, rightly dividing the word of truth"* (II Timothy 2:15). The **humble** shepherds were good Bible students. They were talking "together of the promised Saviour" when "the angel of the Lord came upon them."*

God helped man to keep good records of His Son's **humble** birth. He knew that, especially in the end-time, we would need to study these truths. God will help us to understand the words in the Bible. As we study the **humble** birth of Jesus, we can learn more of what God has revealed.

God has given us the light of His Word that we might share it with those in darkness. Let it not be said of us as it was of the Jews: "With

*The Desire of Ages 47

amazement the heavenly messengers beheld the indifference of that people whom God had called to communicate to the world the light of sacred truth."*

Step 4

Prepare to begin the Language Lesson.

To Begin the Language Lesson

Find an unusual word in the *Strong's Concordance* that you do not know the meaning of. Look it up and discover what it means.

Step 5

Begin the Language Lesson. Cover only what can be understood by your student. Make the lessons a family project by all being involved in part or all of the lesson. These lessons are designed for the whole family.

*The Desire of Ages 44

Steps in Bible Study

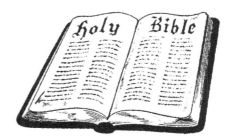

1. Prayer

2. Read the verses/meditate/memorize.

3. Look up key words in *Strong's Concordance* and find their meaning in the Hebrew or Greek dictionary in the back of that book.

4. Cross reference (marginal reference) with other Bible texts. An excellent study tool is *The Treasury of Scripture Knowledge.*

5. Use Bible custom books for more information on the times.

6. Write a summary of what you have learned from those verses.

7. Mark key thoughts in the margin of your Bible.

8. Share your study with others to reinforce the lessons you have learned.

Review Questions

1. In what way did the emperor of Rome become an agent of God? (Luke 2:1, 4, 7)

2. Where did the people go to be taxed? (Luke 2:3)

3. To what city did Joseph and Mary go? Why? (Luke 2:4)

4. Why did they not go to an inn? (Luke 2:7)

5. Who was born that night? (Luke 2:7, 11)

6. In what did His mother wrap Him? ((Luke 2:7)

7. Where did she lay Him? (Luke 2:7)

8. Who were in a field near where Jesus was born, and the only group of people at Bethlehem ready for the great news? (Luke 2:8)

9. What were these shepherds doing? (Luke 2:8)

10. What special thing did the angels do on the night Jesus was born? (Luke 2:9-14)

11. What did the shepherds say to one another when the angels had gone away? (Luke 2:15)

12. Where did they find Jesus? (Luke 2:16)

13. To whom did they tell what they had seen and heard? (Luke 2:17-18)

14. How was their story received? (Luke 2:18)

15. For what did they praise and glorify God? (Luke 2:20)

16. What did Mary ponder in her heart? (Luke 2:19)

17. How many reasons can you think of why the angels should have been interested in the birth of Jesus?

18. Why is Bethlehem called "the city of David?" (Because David had been born there)

19. What lesson do you get from the attitude of the shepherds both before and after the angels' announcement of the birth of Jesus? (They were **humble** and believing of the good news, and eager to share it with others.)

20. Read the genealogies of Christ in Matthew 1:1-17, and Luke 3:23-35. (Note: Luke gives the regal line of Christ through Mary who was descended from Nathan, the son of David, while Matthew gives the regal line through Joseph, who was descended from Solomon, the son of David and heir to the throne.)

Evaluating Your Child's Character

Check the appropriate box for your student's level of development, or your own, as the case may be.

Maturing Nicely (MN), Needs Improvement (NI), Poorly Developed (PD), Absent (A)

Humbleness

1. *"Seest thou a young man wise in his own conceit? there is more hope of a fool than of him."* Is the child teachable, readily and **humbly** submitting themselves to the guidance of those more experienced than themselves?

MN   NI   PD   A
☐   ☐   ☐   ☐

2. Does the child show proper respect to those who are their superiors in knowledge, in station, and in years?

MN   NI   PD   A
☐   ☐   ☐   ☐

3. When praised for something he has done does the child deflect the praise to God or others who played some indirect part in his success?

MN   NI   PD   A
☐   ☐   ☐   ☐

4. Does the child think more highly of himself than he ought to think?

Yes   No
☐   ☐

5. When the child experiences a moral failure of some kind, does it **humble** him or does he seek to justify himself?

6. Does the child prefer showy or modest attire? _____

7. Do your children agree with you?

Yes   No
☐   ☐

8. Does the child find it difficult to admit when he is wrong?

Yes   No
☐   ☐

9. Does the child seldom ask for forgiveness on his own?

Yes   No
☐   ☐

10. Does the child usually respond to conflict in the family with the attitude, "It wasn't my fault?"

Yes   No
☐   ☐

11. Does the child ever choose to "lose face" himself in order to shield another from embarrassment?

MN   NI   PD   A
☐   ☐   ☐   ☐

Answer Key

Page 3

"To be full or satisfied, have enough of"

Page 4

Place I - II

1. From the Word

2. Storehouses, storehouses, storehouse, Bible

3. Words, light

Place II - III

1. *"What saith the Scriptures?"*

2. 214 – depository

3. Over the one who relies on the testimony of God's Word

4. *"The entrance of thy words giveth light; it giveth understanding unto the simple"* (Psalm 119:130).

See page 2.

Page 8

Arise   –   Isaiah 60:1
Communion –   Psalm 77:6
Search   –   John 5:39
Path   –   Psalm 119:105
Promises   –   II Peter 1:4

Page 11

Place I - II

1. *"These were more noble than those in Thessalonica, in that they received the word with all readiness of mind, and searched the Scriptures daily, whether those things were so"* (Acts 17:11).

Student, answer.

2. Teacher, check.
Yes

3. See pages 9-10.
The Mount of Blessings 131

4. Student, answer.

Page 12

1. 2104 – well born; high in rank; generous. (People who study and obey the Word become like this.)

Answer Key

Page 12 continued

2. With "reverence and a sincere desire to know the will of God concerning us."

Angels and the Holy Spirit

3. In His audience chamber

Being in the very presence of God

4. Christ is the Word. His Word imparts life and energy.

5. *"And he **humbled** thee, and suffered thee to hunger, and fed thee with manna, which thou knewest not, neither did thy fathers know; that he might make thee know that man doth not live by bread only, but by every word that proceedeth out of the mouth of the Lord doth man live"* (Deuteronomy 8:3).

1. Sons of thunder

2. God with us

3. The place of the skull

4. King of peace

5. Master

Page 12 continued

6. Son of consolation

7. Sorcerer

8. Damsel

9. Be opened

10. Sent

11. King of righteousness

12. Bitter

13. My God, my God, why hast thou forsaken me?

14. Confused

15. Red

16. Small

17. Booths

18. Burning

19. Not my people

20. No mercy

Page 15

1. Food, no

2. Word, no

3. By studying the Word and obeying it in **humbleness** of spirit

4. Teacher, check.

Page 16

1. Physical, sustained, food, spiritual, sustained, Word of God.
No.

2. See pages 13-14; *"For precept must be upon precept, precept upon precept; line upon line, line upon line; here a little, and there a little"* (Isaiah 28:10).

3. Read and discuss Philippians 4:13.

4. Teacher, check.

Notes

When I Read the Bible Through

I supposed I knew my Bible,
　　Reading piecemeal, hit or miss,
Now a bit of John or Matthew,
　　Now a snatch of Genesis,
Certain chapters of Isaiah,
　　Certain Psalms (the twenty-third),
Twelfth of Romans, first of Proverbs,
　　Yes, I thought I knew the Word!
But I found that though reading
　　Was a different thing to do,
And the way was unfamiliar
　　When I read the Bible through.

You who like to play at Bible,
　　Dip and dabble, here and there,
Just before you kneel a weary,
　　And yawn out a hurried prayer;
You who treat the Crown of Writings
　　As you treat no other book—
Just a paragraph disjointed,
　　Just a crude impatient look—
Try a worthier procedure,
　　Try a broad and steady view:
You will kneel in very rapture
　　When you read the Bible through.
　　　　　—Unknown

Book of Life

Over and over again,
　　No matter which way we turn;
We always find in the book of life
　　Some lesson we have to learn.

Gardening Sheet

Lesson __Four__ Subject __Language__

Title __"Finding and Understanding the Word"__

In Season	Out of Season

In Season

Crop rotation helps the soil and is a valuable aid in producing better, disease-free vegetables.

Crop rotation is simply the practice of planting on any piece of ground a crop totally unrelated to the one previously grown. One year plant beans or peas, next year sweet corn, and follow with tomatoes.

It is rare that a disease affecting corn will affect a tomato crop.

God plants different people at different times in others' lives to witness to them. It is a little like crop rotation. Learn your Bible well so you might be prepared for whomever (crop) God sends to you. Memorize Bible verses while working the soil.

Out of Season

A basic soil mixture for most house plants is 3 parts top soil, 1 part sharp sand, i part peat or leaf molds, add 2 tablespoons (30 ml.) of a balanced plant food for each 1 gallon (3.8 liters) of soil. Mix all thoroughly.

It takes several ingredients in the life to have the best growing conditions. The Bible is the recipe book. Memorize verses.

Mix soil for potting house plants.

Student

Section

"Thy word is a lamp unto my feet,
and a light unto my path."
Psalm 119:105

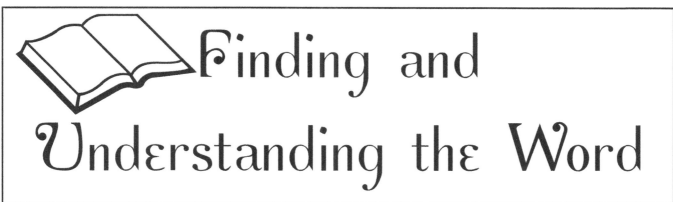

Finding and Understanding the Word

Research
Power in the Word

There is power in the words of the Bible. To **humbly** give a Bible text for an answer to a question is far more effective than an answer you can think up in your own mind.

"But sanctify the Lord God in your hearts: and be ready always to give an answer to every man that asketh you a reason of the hope that is in you with meekness and fear." (I Peter 3:15).

Humbly study the following article to see the importance of the Word in answering another.

Jesus directed His questioners to the great storehouse of knowledge.

Grain Storehouse

What Saith the Scriptures?

"When a question was brought to Christ, His answer was, *'Have ye not read?' 'What saith the Scriptures?'* Christ could have answered every perplexing question brought to Him, but He did not do this. He directed His questioners to the great <u>storehouse</u> of knowledge. He knew that He could not always be with them in human form, and He desired to teach them to make the Word their dependence. *'Search the Scriptures,'* He said. He referred them to His own inspired Word, that when tempted by the enemy they might meet him as He had done, saying *'It is written.'* Thus the enemy could be repulsed; for he has no power over the one who relies on the testimony of God's Word.

"Of the Word of God, the psalmist writes: *'The entrance of thy word giveth light; it giveth understanding to the simple'* (Psalm 119:130). It is a light shining in a dark place. As we search its pages, light enters the heart, illuminating the mind. By this light we see what we ought to be."*

Christ referres people to His own inspired Word. Satan has no power over the one who relies upon the testimony of God's Word.

*Signs of the Times 6-26-1901

A Storehouse

Joseph stored grain (the Word is as seed) in a storehouse. We are told:

"And that food shall be for store to the land against the seven years of famine, which shall be in the land of Egypt; that the land perish not through the famine.

"And the famine was over all the face of the earth: And Joseph opened all the storehouses, and sold unto the Egyptians; and the famine waxed sore in the land of Egypt" (Genesis 41:36, 56).

What does the number seven represent?_____

_____

Jesus is the "Water of Life" and the "Word of Life."

Psalm 33:7 says, *"He gathereth the waters of the sea together as an heap: he layeth up the depth in storehouses."*

God has stored His precious words in the Scriptures just as He stores water in the sea for use when needed.

"Thy Words Giveth Light"

In the Hebrew, "seven" is from the root word which means "to be full or satisfied, have enough of." Seven stamps with completeness or perfection that with which it is used.

7

Review

Place I - II

1. Read Matthew 21:42 (first part).

How did Jesus answer questions asked Him?_____

_____

_____

2. Joseph stored grain in_____

_____

When the people were hungry they came to Joseph and he opened the_____.

The Bible is like a _____

_____

_____

When we are spiritually hungry, we can **humbly** go to the _____ _____ and open it to be fed.

3. Finish this Bible verse.

"The entrance of thy _____ giveth _____; it giveth understanding unto the simple" (Psalm 119:130).

Place II - III

1. How did Jesus **humbly** answer questions that were brought to Him?_____

_____

2. Use the *Strong's Concordance* and define the word, "storehouse."

_____

_____

_____

_____

3. Finish this statement, "Thus the enemy could be repulsed; for he had no power_____

_____

_____."

4. What does Psalm 119:130 say? Explain. _____

_____

_____

_____

Remind

1. As you store food for winter, be reminded how the Word stores precious spiritual food for you to enjoy.

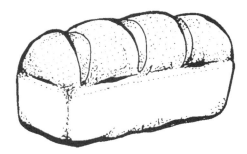

2. When grinding wheat berries into flour for making bread, or when eating bread, or sharing a loaf of bread with another, remember the Bible (Seed), and how it will nourish a person spiritually.

3. When turning a light on or helping to replace light bulbs, think how the Word gives light.

Reinforce

Read the following verses telling what the Bible is to the Christian.

1. Food by which his nature is nourished – I Peter 2:2.

2. Preservative against sin – Psalm 119:11.

3. Quickens the soul – Psalm 119:50.

4. Enriches the soul – Psalm 119:72.

5. Imparts superior wisdom – Psalm 119:98.

6. Brings peace to him – Psalm 119:165.

7. Plea for help – Psalm 119:175.

8. His delight – Psalm 119:16.

The Bible is stored with spiritual food.

Research
Our Counsel and Guide

"We see in the Word, warnings and promises, with God behind them all. We are invited to <u>search</u> this Word for aid when brought into difficult places. If we do not consult the guidebook at every step, inquiring, 'Is this the way of the Lord?' our words and acts will be tainted by selfishness. We shall forget God, and walk in paths that He has not chosen for us."*

"Search the scriptures; for in them ye think ye have eternal life: and they are they which testify of me" (John 5:39).

"God's Word is full of precious <u>promises</u> and helpful counsel. It is infallible; for God can not err. It has help for every circumstance and condition of life, and God looks on with sadness when His children turn from it to human aid."*

"Whereby are given unto us exceeding great and precious promises: that by these ye might be partakers of the divine nature, having escaped the corruption that is in the world through lust" (II Peter 1:4).

"He who communes with God through the Scriptures will be ennobled and sanctified. As he reads the inspired record of the Saviour's love, his heart is melted in tenderness and contrition. He is filled with a desire to be like the Master, to live a life of loving service."*

"I call to remembrance my song in the night: I commune with mine own heart: and my spirit made diligent search" (Psalm 77:6).

Reflect

"Words are things; and a small drop of ink,

falling like dew upon a thought,

produces that which makes thousands, perhaps millions, think."

—Byron

Signs of the Times 6-26-1901

"Great <u>light</u> shone forth from the patriarchs and prophets. Glorious things were spoken of Zion, the city of God. Thus the Lord designs that the light shall shine forth through His followers today. If the saints of the Old Testament bore such a bright testimony of loyalty, should we not today, upon whom is shining the accumulated light of centuries, arise and shine? The glory of the prophecies sheds light on our <u>pathway</u>. Type has met antitype in the death of God's Son. Christ has risen from the dead, proclaiming over the tomb, *'I am the resurrection and the life.'* He has sent His Spirit into our world to bring all things to our remembrance. By a miracle of His power He has preserved His written Word through the ages. Shall we not, then, make this Word our constant study, learning from it God's purpose for us?"*

Reflect

"Arise, shine;
for thy light is come,
and the glory of the Lord is
risen upon thee."
Isaiah 60:1

"Thy word is a lamp
unto my feet,
and a light
unto my path."
Psalm 119:105

"Great Light Shone Forth From the Patriarchs and Prophets."

Signs of the Times 6-26-1901

Review
Place I - II - III

Match these verses with these words.
A **Place I** student may look the verses up. Use a ruler.

arise	II Peter 1:4
commune	John 5:39
search	Psalm 77:6
path	Isaiah 60:1
promises	Psalm 119:105

Thy Word
Read these verse.
Psalm 119:130

Would you be happy? Read the Word, Psalm 119:162; Jeremiah 15:16; and John 15:11.

Would you be wise? Read the Word, Proverbs 1:1, 7; I Corinthians 2:1, 16; Colossians 1:9.

Would you be fruitful? Read the Word, Galatians 5:22-23; Luke 8:11, 15; romans 10:17.

Would you be holy? Read the Word, Psalm 119:9, 11; Ephesians 5:27-27; John 15:3.

Would you be a successful servant? Read the Word, Joshua 1:7-8; II timothy 2:15; Hebrews 4:12.

Would you have eternal life? Read the Word, Luke 16:22, 31; Acts 11:14; I Peter 1:23, 25.

Reinforce

1. As you **humbly** search God's Word, thank Him for it.

2. Make a list of promises for an area in your life that you need special help with.

3. Pray and then meditate on one verse each day. It is always good to know a few verses about **humbleness**.

4. As you observe the sun rising, or walk on a path, be reminded of God's Word (Psalm 119:105).

5. Try to find some of the promises the **humble** shepherds might have been talking about the night the angel of the Lord visited them.

Research
Why More Noble?

"The <u>Bereans</u> were commended as being more noble than those of Thessalonica, in that they received the Word with all readiness of mind, and searched the Scriptures daily. They did not search the Bible from curiosity, but that they might learn in regard to Christ. Daily, they compared Scripture with Scripture; and as they searched, heavenly intelligences were beside them, enlightening their minds and impressing their hearts."

"These were more noble than those in Thessalonica, in that they received the word with all readiness of mind, and searched the scriptures daily, whether those things were so" (Acts 17:11).

"We are to open the Word of God with reverence, and with a sincere desire to know the will of God concerning us. Then the heavenly <u>angels</u> will direct our search. God speaks to us in His Word. We are in the <u>audience chamber</u> of the Most High, in the very presence of God. Christ enters the heart. The Holy Spirit takes of the things of

The Bereans studied the Scriptures.

God, and shows them to us. We see more clearly the greatness of God's love and the fullness of His salvation. We appreciate more fully His gracious design to make us partakers in the heavenly firm. We are drawn into full sympathy with the plans of God. His secret is with us, and He shows us His covenant."*

" *'Knock.'* We come to God by special invitation, and He waits to welcome us to His audience chamber. The first disciples who followed Jesus were not satisfied with a hurried conversation with Him by the way; they said, *'Rabbi,...where dwellest thou?...They came and saw where he dwelt, and abode with him that day'* (John 1:38-39). So we may be admitted into closest intimacy and communion with God. *'He that dwelleth in the secret place of the Most High shall abide under the shadow of the Almighty'* (Psalm 91:1). Let those who desire the blessing of God knock and wait at the door of mercy with firm assurance, saying, For Thou, O Lord, hast said, *'Everyone that asketh receiveth; and he that seeketh findeth; and to him that knocketh it shall be opened.'* "**

"...The greatest victories which are gained to the cause are not by labored argument, ample facilities, abundance of influence, and plenty of means; but they are those victories which are gained in the audience chamber with God, when earnest, agonizing faith lays hold upon the mighty arm of power."***

"The life of Christ, that gives life to the world, is in His Word. It was by His word that Jesus healed disease and cast out demons; by His Word He stilled the sea and raised the dead; and the people bore witness that His Word was with power. He spoke the Word of God, as He had spoken through all the prophets and teachers of the Old Testament. The whole Bible is a manifestation of Christ, and the Saviour desires to fix the faith of His followers on the Word. When His visible presence should be withdrawn, the Word must be their source of Power. Like their Master, they were to live by *'every word that proceedeth out of the mouth of God.'* "*

*The Signs of the Times 3-28-1906 **Thoughts From the Mount of Blessings 131 ***4 Testimonies 443-444

"In the beginning was the Word, and the Word was with God, and the Word was God.

"The same was in the beginning with God.

"All things were made by him; and without him was not any thing made that was made.

"In him was life; and the life was the light of men" (John 1:1-4).

*"And he **humbled** thee, and suffered thee to hunger, and fed thee with manna, which thou knewest not, neither did thy fathers know; that he might make thee know that man doth not live by bread only, but by every word that proceedeth out of the mouth of the Lord doth man live"* (Deuteronomy 8:3).

"He...

fed thee with manna...."

Review
Place I - II

1. Who were the Bereans?_____

_____

_____

Are you like a **humble** Berean?

_____

2. Explain Hebrews 1:14.

_____

_____

_____

_____

Do we need the angels' help when we study the Word?_____

3. What is an audience chamber?_____

_____

_____

4. Read John 1:1-4. Did you know that His Word, the Scriptures, can give you spiritual life?_____

_____

Review
Place II - III

1. Look up the word "noble" in the *Strong's Concordance*. What does it mean?_____

_____

_____

2. How are we to open the Word?_____

_____

_____

Then who will be by our sides to direct our search?_____

3. Where are we when we **humbly** study the words of God?

_____

_____

Where is that?_____

_____

_____

4. Explain this statement, "The life of Christ, that gives life to the world, is in His Word."

5. Like our Master, how are we to live?_____

_____

(Deuteronomy 8:3)

Scripture Translates Itself
Translate these words from Scripture.

1. Boanerges (Mark 3:17)
2. Immanuel (Matthew 1:23)
3. Golgotha (Matthew 27:33)
4. King of Salem (Hebrews 7:2)
5. Rabboni or Rabbi (John 1:38; 20:16)
6. Barnabas (Acts 4:36)
7. Elymas (Acts 13:8)
8. Talitha (Mark 5:41)
9. Ephphatha (Mark 7:34)
10. Siloam (John 9:7)
11. Melchizedek (Hebrews 7:2)
12. Marah (Exodus 15:23)
13. Eloi, eloi, lama sabachthani (Mark 15:34)
14. Babel (Genesis 11:9)
15. Edom (Genesis 25:30)
16. Zoar (Genesis 19:22)
17. Succoth (Genesis 33:17)
18. Taberah (Numbers 11:3)
19. Lo-ammi (Hosea 1:9)
20. Lo-ruhamah (Hosea 1:6)

Reinforce
Place I - II - III

1. Daily learn to be like the noble Bereans, as you learn more ways to study the Word.

2. Find an "audience chamber," a place where you can talk to God and be all alone with Him.

3. Thank God for your angel friends. If you have not read the book, *It Must Have Been an Angel*, you might like to do so at this time.

4. In **humbleness**, obey every word of God. Each chore you are asked to do, do quickly with joy in your heart.

The Shepherds
Obeyed God's Word

Research
Sustained

"As our physical life is sustained by food, so our spiritual life is sustained by the Word of God. As we must eat for ourselves in order to obtain nourishment, so we must receive the Word for ourselves. We are not to obtain it merely through the medium of another's mind. We should carefully study the Bible, asking God for the aid of the Holy Spirit, that we may understand His Word. We should take one verse, and concentrate the mind on the task of ascertaining the thought that God has in that verse for us. We should dwell upon the thought until it becomes our own, and we know *'what saith the Lord.'*"*

Remember our verse in Deuteronomy 8:3—

*"And he **humbled** thee, and suffered thee to hunger, and fed thee with manna, which thou knewest not, neither did thy fathers know; that he might make thee know that man doth not live by bread only, but by every word that proceedeth out of the mouth of the Lord doth man live."*

> **Carefully Study the Bible**

*Signs of the Times 3-28-1906

"For precept must be upon precept, precept upon precept; line upon line, line upon line; here a little, and there a little" (Isaiah 28:10).

Each word is important!

"In the Bible we have in clear lines the revelation of God's character, of His dealings with men, and the great work of redemption. Here is open before us the history of patriarchs and prophets, and other holy men of old. They were men *'subject to like passions as we are.'* We see how they struggled through discouragements like our own, how they fell under temptation as we have done, and yet took heart again and conquered through the grace of God; and, beholding, we are encouraged in our strivings after righteousness. As we read of the precious experience granted them, of the light and love and blessing it was their privilege to enjoy, and of the work they wrought through the grace given them, the Spirit that inspired them kindles a flame of holy emulation in our hearts, and a desire to be like them in character—like them, to walk with God."*

"Brethren, I count not myself to have apprehended: but this one thing I do, forgetting those things which are behind, and reaching forth unto those things which are before" (Philippians 3:13).

"Teach me thy way, O Lord; I will walk in thy truth: unite my heart to fear thy name" (Psalm 86:11).

Read good books.
Good reading prepares the mind for right thinking:
and from right thinking spring the noble character
and well-ordered life.
The Bible is the very best book to read!

---

*Signs of the Times 3-28-1906

Review
Place I - II

1. What main thing sustains our physical life?_____

Can another eat for us?_____

2. What sustains our spiritual life?_____

_____

Can another study for us?_____

3. How can you walk with God? _____

_____

4. Your teacher can dictate your spelling words. Spell, define, and use them in a sentence.

Place I	**Place II**
_____	_____
_____	_____
_____	_____
_____	_____
_____	_____
_____	_____
_____	_____

Review
Place II - III

1. Finish this statement, "As our _____ life is

_____ by _____, so our _____ life is

_____ by the _____ _____ _____."

Can another eat for us? _____

2. How are we to study? _____

_____

3. What does Philippians 4:13 say? _____

_____

4. Teacher can dictate the spelling words. Spell, give the literal and spiritual definition, and write a sentence using the word as it relates to the lesson.

Place II

_____

_____

_____

_____

_____

_____

_____

Place III

_____

_____

_____

_____

_____

_____

_____

Reinforce

1. As you fix a meal or go to the store to purchase food, be reminded how the Word sustains our spiritual life.

2. Memorize Scriptures so that as you go about your duties you can think about each word and what they mean. Memorizing verses can be like storing seed in the storehouse for times of famine.

3. As you take a walk, think how you can **humbly** "walk with God."

4. Read the stories and poem on the next pages, and "Mark Your Bible."

Memorizing Scripture

"...Precept upon precept; line upon line, line upon line, here a little, and there a little."

Reflect
Summary

• To answer a person with the Word we need to understand the words we use from the Scriptures.

• Search out the meanings of the words in the Scriptures.

• As we seek understanding of the words angels and the Holy Spirit will assist us.

• Each word in Scripture is important.

• Do page 7 from the booklet, *Bible Study*. This will continue to teach you how to define the words in the Bible.

My Bible and I

We've traveled together, my Bible and I,
Through all kinds of weather, with smile or with sigh,
In sorrow or sunshine, in tempest or calm,
Thy friendship unchanging, my lamp and my psalm.

We've traveled together, my Bible and I,
When life had grown weary, and death e'en was nigh,
But all through the darkness of mist and of wrong,
I found thee a solace, a prayer, and a song.

So now who shall part us, my Bible and I,
Shall ism, or schism, or new lights that try?
Shall shadow for substance or stone for good bread
Supplant its sound wisdom, give folly instead?

Ah, no my dear Bible, revealer of light,
Thou sword of the spirit, put error to flight;
And still through life's journey, until my last sigh,
We'll travel together, my Bible and I.

"Feasting On God's Word"

"Where have you been reading this morning, uncle?"

"Well, Sandy," said the old man, "I have been getting a wonderful feast yesterday and today out of the last two verses of the eighth chapter of Romans."

"And have you not read any more than these two verses in two days?" asked Sandy, with a little surprise.

"O surely, surely," said the uncle. "I have been going over the breadth of the surface elsewhere, but I have been trying to sink a mine down there at the end of Romans. And I'm not down at the big nuggets yet. You see, I do the same thing with these verses that I do with these special homemade cough drops your good aunt made for me. I am having trouble with my lungs and these cough drops ease my coughing spells. There is nothing bad in them, just something to soothe the tickle in my throat. Mary now and then puts one of them in her mouth, but she gives it just a chew or two and it is all gone. But I lay mine in my cheek and let it alone. That way it slowly melts and does me good for half a day. Did you know that many people do the same thing with the Bible? They gallop over a chapter and it's done; but that seems like a waste to me. I like to take a sweet passage and sup on it—a verse or a word, maybe—and 'let it lie in my cheek and melt,' and fill my soul with its sweetness, for a day or a week or a month at a time." Did you ever try this way of feasting on God's Word?

"Preciousness of the Bible"

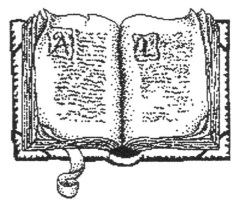

Long ago, there was a **humble** old man in the West Indies who lived quite a long distance from a certain missionary. But the man was exceedingly interested in learning to read the Bible, so he made the long trip to the missionary regularly for a lesson. He was not making much progress in learning to read, so his teacher, almost disheartened, finally hinted his fears that his labors would be lost, and asked the man, "Had you not better give up trying?" "no, massa, me die;" replied the **humble** man, and pointing his finger to John 3:16 (*"God so loved the world, that he gave his only begotten Son, that whosoever believeth in him should not perish, but have everlasting life"*), he said with touching emphasis, "It is worth all de labor, to be able to read dat one single verse."

 # Mark Your Bible

Power of the Word

1. All the power of God is in His Word.

Hebrews 4:12 – *"For the word of God is quick, and powerful, and sharper than any two edged sword, piercing even to the dividing asunder of soul and spirit, and of the joints and marrow, and is a discerner of the thoughts and intents of the heart."*

2. God's Word, hidden in the heart, will shield from sin.

Psalm 119:11 – *"Thy word have I hid in mine heart, that I might not sin against thee."*

3. Jesus used the Word to resist Satan's temptations.

Matthew 4:8-11 – *"Again, the devil taketh him up into an exceeding high mountain, and sheweth him all the kingdoms of the world, and the glory of them; And saith unto him, All these things will I give thee, if thou wilt fall down and worship me. Then saith Jesus unto him, Get thee hence, Satan: for it is written, Thou shalt worship the Lord thy God, and him only shalt thou serve. Then the devil leaveth him, and behold, angels came and ministered unto him."*

3. God's Word is healing.

Psalm 107:20 – *"He sent his word, and healed thee, and delivered them from their destructions."*

4. There is creative power in God's Word.

Psalm 33:6 – *"By the word of the Lord were the heavens made; and all the host of them by the breath of his mouth."*

5. God's Word has life-sustaining power in it.

Deuteronomy 8:3 – *"And he **humbled** thee and suffered thee to hunger, and fed thee with manna, which thou knewest not, neither did thy fathers know; that he might make thee know that man doth not live by bread only, but by every word that proceedeth out of the mouth of the Lord doth man live."*

> **"Much wisdom often goes with fewest words."**
> —Sophocles

"Seek Us a Book"

"Go seek a Book! Oh go seek a Book! let us not go back empty!" This was the plea of a Bechuana woman in South Africa, who brought her boy to Dr. Moffat asking for a copy of the Bible which he had translated into Bechuana. The two had walked fifteen miles in search of the missionary, but when they found him, he only shook his head and said:

"There is not a Bible left."

"I once borrowed a copy," the woman said. "But the owner has come and taken it away and now I sit with my family sorrowful because we have no Book to talk to us. My boy here can read and he is teaching me to read. We live far from anyone else, and we have not one to teach us but the Book. So my boy reads to us and I pray. Oh," she added, "go seek a Book! Oh father, Oh elder brother, go seek a book for us! Surely there is one to be found. Let us not go back empty."

When Dr. Moffat at last got a copy for them, both the lad and his mother greatly rejoiced.

On A Rubbish Heap

A young man in Argentina who possessed a Bible that his father had given him, became engaged to a girl from another faith. Her confessor informed her that before she could marry, the bridegroom's Bible must be burned. She told her fiance this ultimatum, so the young man very reluctantly took his Bible, and as he had not courage to burn it, left it on a rubbish heap. A woman passing the rubbish heap saw a book which looked new, took it home with her, examined it. She said, "from that memorable day all of us have read it, and the reading has resulted in the conversion of several of our family." She was thankful that she had been led to pass by that rubbish heap and to secure such a treasure.

Outline of School Program

Age	Grade	Program
Birth through Age 7	Babies Kindergarten and Pre-school	*Family Bible Lessons* (This includes: Bible, Science–Nature, and Character)
Age 8	First Grade	*Family Bible Lessons* (This includes: Bible, Science–Nature, and Character) + Language Program (*Writing and Spelling Road to Reading and Thinking* [WSRRT])
Age 9-14 or 15	Second through Eighth Grade	*The Desire of all Nations* (This includes: Health, Mathematics, Music, Science–Nature, History/Geography/Prophecy, Language, and Voice–Speech) + Continue using WSRRT
Ages 15 or 16-19	Ninth through Twelfth Grade	9 – *Cross and Its Shadow I* * + Appropriate Academic Books 10 – *Cross and Its Shadow II* * + Appropriate Academic Books 11 – *Daniel the Prophet* * + Appropriate Academic Books 12 – *The Seer of Patmos* * (Revelation) + Appropriate Academic Books *or you could continue using *The Desire of Ages*
Ages 20-25	College	Apprenticeship

Made in the USA
Monee, IL
21 August 2022

11941358R00026